Excellence
in Scientific
Enquiry

Year 5

By Graham Peacock

RISING★STARS

Rising Stars UK Ltd., 76 Farnaby Road, Bromley, BR1 4BH

Website: **www.risingstars-uk.com**

Published 2003
Reprinted 2004

Text, design and layout ©Rising Stars UK Ltd.

Editorial: Tanya Solomons

Concept design: Burville Riley

Design: Ken Vail Graphic Design

Illustration copyright ©Louisa Burville-Riley

Cover photo ©Richard Wahlstrom/Getty Images

British Library Cataloguing in Publication Data

A CIP record for this book is available from the British Library.

ISBN 1-904591-25-6

Printed by Wyndeham Gait, Grimsby, UK

Contents

How to use this book   4

Scientific Enquiry – what you should know?   6

Unit 1 – *Keeping healthy* – pulse rate   8

Unit 2 – *Keeping healthy* – eating the right stuff   10

Unit 1 and 2 summary   12

Unit 3 – *Life cycles* – germination   14

Unit 4 – *Life cycles* – scattering seeds   16

Unit 3 and 4 summary   18

Unit 5 – *Gases around us* – evaporation   20

Unit 6 – *Gases around us* – gases spread   22

Unit 5 and 6 summary   24

Unit 7 – *Changing stage* – melting   26

Unit 8 – *Changing state* – condensation   28

Unit 7 and 8 summary   30

Unit 9 – *Earth, Sun and Moon* – length of shadows   32

Unit 10 – *Earth, Sun and Moon* – sunset times   34

Unit 9 and 10 summary   36

Unit 11 – *Changing sounds* – muffling sounds   38

Unit 12 – *Changing sounds* – pitch of sounds   40

Unit 11 and 12 summary   42

Answers   44

How to use this book

The *Excellence in Scientific Enquiry* series is designed to help you to master the investigative skills and to apply what you know about science to practical problems.

The introduction

This section introduces the topic that you will be studying and gives you a basic idea of the skills and content covered.

The investigation

Here the investigation is described and you are provided with all the data you need to answer the questions on the following page.

Approaching the investigation

This is the important bit! The flow chart can be used with any investigation and gives you a way of looking at all investigations in the future.
If you can answer these key questions, you have covered the skills you need to know. The same questions are important when you are doing investigations in class too!

Keeping healthy – pulse rate

Class 5N have been studying what happens to their pulse rate when they exercise.

The investigation

Class 5N wanted to find out how pulse rates change.

The class predicted that skipping would raise their pulse rate most. They thought that skipping is harder exercise than walking or jogging.

Pulse rate is measured in beats per minute.

Mr Newton attached a pulse meter to Laura's hand.

Pulse meters show the number of beats per minute.

It measured her pulse rate:
- when sitting
- after walking
- after jogging
- after skipping

These are the results:

	Pulse rate when sitting	Pulse rate after walking	Pulse rate after jogging	Pulse rate after skipping
Laura	80	86	95	112

Approaching the investiga

1. What did the class want to fir out?
   How different exercise affecte Laura's pulse rate.
2. How did they create a fair tes
   They asked the same child to the exercises.
   She did each exercise for the length of time.
   The pulse was measured in th same way each time.
3. What equipment did they use
   Skipping rope
   Pulse meter
   Stopwatch
4. How did they carry out the tes
   They measured her pulse rate soon as she finished each act
5. What did they predict?
   The pulse rate will go highes skipping.
6. What factor did they change?
   The exercise Laura did.
7. What factor did they measure
   Laura's pulse rate.
8. What did they find out?
   Exercise alters Laura's pulse

Investigate! Hints and tips

★ If you do not have a pulse rate meter, practise finding the pulse rate using your fingers.
★ Test your pulse rate before exercising.
★ Make sure each person does the same exercise.
★ Test your pulse rate as soon as you have finished exercising.

Investigate! Hints and tips

The hints and tips section gives you useful ideas for completing the questions on the other page. They also give advice about completing the investigation in your class.

The questions

The questions get harder as you move down the page.

- Section 1 questions are often multiple choice and cover the basic elements of the investigation.
- Section 2 questions will often ask you for more information about the investigation.
- Section 3 questions usually relate to data handling and you will often have to complete a graph or chart to get full marks.

Activity

This activity will help you to remember the key points of the subject.

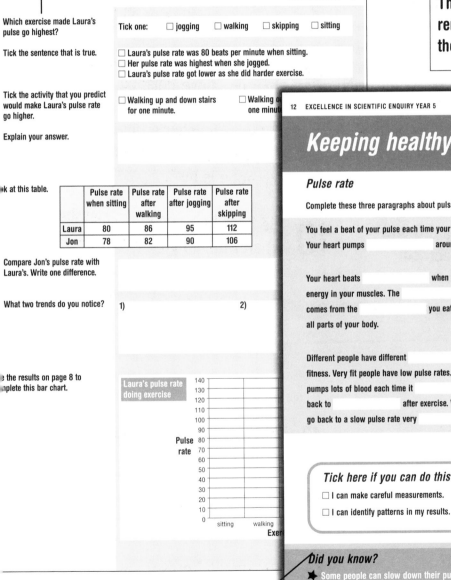

Which exercise made Laura's pulse go highest?

Tick one: ☐ jogging   ☐ walking   ☐ skipping   ☐ sitting

Tick the sentence that is true.

☐ Laura's pulse rate was 80 beats per minute when sitting.
☐ Her pulse rate was highest when she jogged.
☐ Laura's pulse rate got lower as she did harder exercise.

Tick the activity that you predict would make Laura's pulse rate go higher.

☐ Walking up and down stairs for one minute.   ☐ Walking ... one minut...

Explain your answer.

...k at this table.

	Pulse rate when sitting	Pulse rate after walking	Pulse rate after jogging	Pulse rate after skipping
Laura	80	86	95	112
Jon	78	82	90	106

Compare Jon's pulse rate with Laura's. Write one difference.

What two trends do you notice?   1)   2)

...e the results on page 8 to ...mplete this bar chart.

Laura's pulse rate doing exercise

Pulse rate
140
130
120
110
100
90
80
70
60
50
40
30
20
10
0
sitting   walking
Exer...

Keeping healthy – summary

Pulse rate

Complete these three paragraphs about pulse rate.

You feel a beat of your pulse each time your _____ beats.
Your heart pumps _____ around the body.

Your heart beats _____ when you exercise because you need oxygen and
energy in your muscles. The _____ is taken from your lungs. Energy
comes from the _____ you eat. It is taken by the _____ to
all parts of your body.

Different people have different _____ rates. Part of the reason for this is
fitness. Very fit people have low pulse rates. This is because their _____
pumps lots of blood each time it _____. It takes time for pulse rates to go
back to _____ after exercise. Very _____ people will
go back to a slow pulse rate very _____.

Tick here if you can do this now!

☐ I can make careful measurements.   ☐ I can show data in charts.

☐ I can identify patterns in my results.   ☐ I can explain my conclusions.

Did you know?

★ Some people can slow down their pulse rate just by thinking. They can control their body so that their heart rate slows right down. These very skilful people might do this if they are performing tricks that involve them having very little air to breathe.

★ Hibernating animals also slow down their pulse rate. Animals like bats and polar bears slow down their heart during the winter so they do not use up all their food stored as fat. Their body temperature falls but they keep just warm enough to avoid freezing.

Skills checklist

Tick off the skills when you can do them.

Did you know?

This section gives you some interesting facts about the subject.

Scientific Enquiry – what you need to kno

Top 10 Safety Hints

Remember these key rules when carrying out investigations:

1 Always listen to your teacher's instructions.

2 Follow written instructions carefully.

3 If you don't understand any instructions, ask your teacher for help.

4 Take care when CUTTING or HEATING materials.

5 Make sure your hands are dry and keep water away from electrical equipment.

6 Don't run near flames or sharp instruments.

7 Treat your classmates with care and consideration at all times.

8 Always clear up the equipment when you have finished with it.

9 Tell your teacher if anything goes wrong with the investigation or someone is hurt.

10 Tie back hair and loose clothing when working on investigations.

1 What do I want to find out?

2 What can I predict?

3 How can I make a fair test?

4 What do I need to change?

5 What do I need to keep the same?

6 How should I record my results?

7 What have I found out?

8 How should I present my findings?

9 What else could I test?

10 Can I explain my ideas?

Scientists you should know

Edward Jenner 1749–1823

He was a doctor from Gloucester who invented a vaccination for smallpox. This disease had previously killed thousands of people all over the world. By giving people a small dose of another illness (called cowpox) he stopped them getting smallpox.

Louis Pasteur 1822–1895

He invented modern biology and a cure for rabies. Pasteur realised that small organisms called germs carried diseases. Knowing this, he invented a way to keep milk fresh by destroying all the germs in the milk. This is called pasteurisation.

Isaac Newton 1642–1727

Newton was the first person to discover that our tides are affected by the Moon. He also wrote much of what we know today about gravity.

Marie Curie 1867–1934

Curie discovered radium and won the Nobel Prize twice. She invented X-ray vans in the First World War to help save soldiers' lives.

Keeping healthy – pulse rate

Class 5N have been studying what happens to their pulse rate when they exercise.

The investigation

Class 5N wanted to find out how pulse rates change.

The class predicted that skipping would raise their pulse rate most. They thought that skipping is harder exercise than walking or jogging.

Pulse rate is measured in beats per minute.

Mr Newton attached a pulse meter to Laura's hand.

Pulse meters show the number of beats per minute.

It measured her pulse rate:
- when sitting
- after walking
- after jogging
- after skipping

These are the results:

	Pulse rate when sitting	Pulse rate after walking	Pulse rate after jogging	Pulse rate after skipping
Laura	80	86	95	112

Approaching the investigation

1 What did the class want to find out?
How different exercise affected Laura's pulse rate.

2 How did they create a fair test?
They asked the same child to do the exercises.
She did each exercise for the same length of time.
The pulse was measured in the same way each time.

3 What equipment did they use?
Skipping rope
Pulse meter
Stopwatch

4 How did they carry out the test?
They measured her pulse rate as soon as she finished each activity.

5 What did they predict?
The pulse rate will go highest when skipping.

6 What factor did they change?
The exercise Laura did.

7 What factor did they measure?
Laura's pulse rate.

8 What did they find out?
Exercise alters Laura's pulse rate.

Investigate! Hints and tips

★ If you do not have a pulse rate meter, practise finding the pulse rate using your fingers.

★ Test your pulse rate before exercising.

★ Make sure each person does the same exercise.

★ Test your pulse rate as soon as you have finished exercising.

a) Which exercise made Laura's pulse go highest?

Tick one: ☐ jogging   ☐ walking   ☐ skipping   ☐ sitting

b) Tick the sentence that is true.

☐ Laura's pulse rate was 80 beats per minute when sitting.
☐ Her pulse rate was highest when she jogged.
☐ Laura's pulse rate got lower as she did harder exercise.

c) Tick the activity that you predict would make Laura's pulse rate go higher.

☐ Walking up and down stairs for one minute.   ☐ Walking on the flat for one minute.

d) Explain your answer.

2 Look at this table.

	Pulse rate when sitting	Pulse rate after walking	Pulse rate after jogging	Pulse rate after skipping
Laura	80	86	95	112
Jon	78	82	90	106

a) Compare Jon's pulse rate with Laura's. Write one difference.

b) What two trends do you notice?

1)   2)

3 Use the results on page 8 to complete this bar chart.

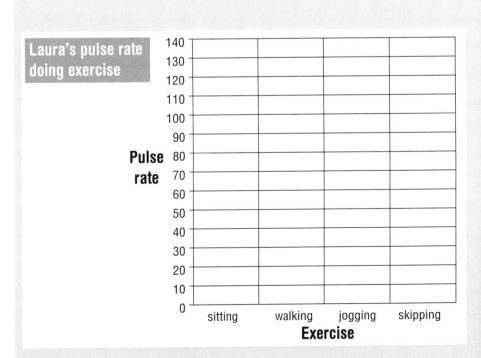

Laura's pulse rate doing exercise

Pulse rate

140
130
120
110
100
90
80
70
60
50
40
30
20
10
0

sitting   walking   jogging   skipping

Exercise

Keeping healthy – eating the right stuff

Class 5N are studying their diet. They ask people in their class how many biscuits and bags of crisps they eat each day.

The investigation

Class 5N did a survey of some of the foods each person ate in two days.

They counted:
- the number of bags of crisps
- the number of biscuits

The children wonder if it is fair to compare:
- a bag of crisps with a single biscuit
- big biscuits with small ones

They counted the bags of crisps and biscuits over two days.

They worked out an average.

Here is part of the results:

	Day 1		Day 2		Average for each day	
	Crisps	Biscuits	Crisps	Biscuits	Crisps	Biscuits
Jon	3	3	5	1	4	2
Teri	4	2	2	6	3	4

Approaching the investigation

1. **What did the class want to find out?**
   How many biscuits and bags of crisps they were eating each day.

2. **How did they create a fair survey?**
   They asked each person what they ate over two days.

3. **What equipment did they use?**
   None

4. **How did they carry out the survey?**
   They kept a record of the biscuits and crisps they ate.

5. **What factor did they measure?**
   The number of biscuits and bags of crisps they ate in two days.
   They took an average.

6. **What did they find out?**
   Jon eats lots of crisps and biscuits. Teri eats fewer crisps but more biscuits.

Investigate! Hints and tips

★ Agree before you start what counts as a biscuit and if big bags of crisps count for more than small ones.

★ Agree what a piece of fruit is.

★ Use a computer spreadsheet to record the numbers – it will do the boring bits like adding up and making the chart for you.

1

a) Who ate the most biscuits?
   Tick one name.

☐ Jon   ☐ Teri

b) The survey only lasted two days.
   Tim thinks they should do it for
   a week. Say why this is a good
   idea.

2

The children want to survey the
amount of fruit eaten.

a) Would it be fair to compare one
   grape with an apple?
   Circle your answer.

Yes   No

b) Explain your answer.

3

Use the results on page 10 to
complete this chart.
Look at the average of crisps and
biscuits Jon and Teri eat each day.
Make a bar chart to show this.

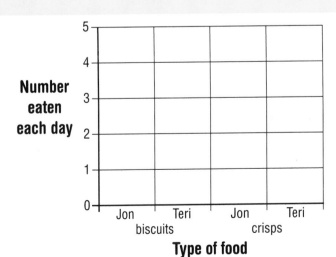

Keeping healthy – summary

Pulse rate

Complete these three paragraphs about pulse rate.

You feel a beat of your pulse each time your _____ beats.
Your heart pumps _____ around the body.

Your heart beats _____ when you exercise because you need oxygen and
energy in your muscles. The _____ is taken from your lungs. Energy
comes from the _____ you eat. It is taken by the _____ to
all parts of your body.

Different people have different _____ rates. Part of the reason for this is
fitness. Very fit people have low pulse rates. This is because their _____
pumps lots of blood each time it _____. It takes time for pulse rates to go
back to _____ after exercise. Very _____ people will
go back to a slow pulse rate very _____

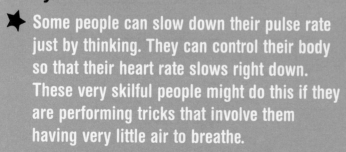

Tick here if you can do this now!

☐ I can make careful measurements.   ☐ I can show data in charts.

☐ I can identify patterns in my results.   ☐ I can explain my conclusions.

Did you know?

★ Some people can slow down their pulse rate just by thinking. They can control their body so that their heart rate slows right down. These very skilful people might do this if they are performing tricks that involve them having very little air to breathe.

★ Hibernating animals also slow down their pulse rate. Animals like bats and polar bears slow down their heart during the winter so they do not use up all their food stored as fat. Their body temperature falls but they keep just warm enough to avoid freezing.

Eating the right stuff

★ Biscuits are made with a lot of fat and sugar.

★ Crisps are made with a lot of fat and salt.

★ Too much fat can make us overweight.

★ Too much sugar can make our teeth decay.

1. Underline in red the ingredients of biscuits.
2. Underline in blue the ingredients of crisps.
3. Underline in green one bad thing that happens if we eat too much sugar.

Answer these questions:

4. Which of these two foods contains fat and salt?

5. Which of these two foods contains lots of sugar?

Most doctors think that we should eat more fruit and vegetables. There are several reasons for this. Fruit and vegetables have lots of fibre to keep your intestines working properly. They have lots of vitamins to keep skin healthy. They fill you up but will not make you fat.

Biscuits and crisps are tasty but we should only eat a few of them. Crisps and biscuits both have a lot of fat in them. Eating fat can make us overweight. Biscuits contain lots of sugar, which may also make us overweight. The salt in crisps makes us thirsty, causes our kidneys to work very hard and might cause poor health as we get older.

1. Write in a title for each of these two paragraphs.
2. Circle the three organs of the body that are mentioned.
3. Underline the food that contains a lot of salt.

Tick here if you can do this now!

☐ I can use results to draw conclusions.

☐ I can identify patterns in results.

☐ I can evaluate the evidence and the activity.

☐ I can represent data in charts.

☐ I can relate observations and conclusions to scientific understanding.

Did you know?

★ In the past Eskimo people ate very little fruit or vegetables as there is little growing in the northern lands where they live. Doctors are puzzled about how they stayed healthy.

Life cycles – germination

Class 5N want to find out the conditions in which seeds sprout most quickly.

The investigation

Class 5N put beans in two pots of compost. They put them in two places.

- in a warm cupboard
- in a cool cupboard

The pots are the same size.

The compost is the same in both pots.

Both pots are given the same amount of water.

They predicted that beans need both warmth and water to sprout.

Here are the results:

warm	4 days to sprout
cool	7 days to sprout

Approaching the investigation

1 What did the class want to find out?
They wanted to find the best conditions to sprout beans.

2 What equipment did they use?
Compost
Pots
Seeds

3 What factors did they keep the same?
The pots are the same size.
The compost is the same in both pots.
Both pots are given the same amount of water.

4 What factor did they measure?
They measured the number of days it took the seeds to sprout.

5 How did they record their results?
In a table.

6 What did they find out?
Seeds germinate more quickly in warm conditions than in cool conditions.

Investigate! Hints and tips

★ Carry out the investigation yourself to see whether beans or peas sprout more quickly.

★ Put two or three seeds of each kind in the pot.
★ Do not keep the compost too damp.

★ Make sure you use the same compost in each pot.
★ Make sure you cover the seeds with compost.

1

a) In which conditions did the seeds germinate most quickly?

Tick one: ☐ Warm   ☐ Cool

b) How long did it take the beans to sprout in the cool place?

2

The class wanted to find out if beans or peas germinate most quickly.

a) Describe a test they could do to find out.

b) In this test which four conditions would you keep the same?

c) What factor would you measure?

3

Use the results on page 14 to complete this bar chart.

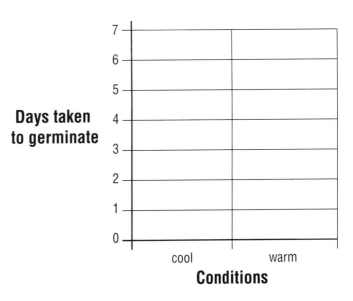

Life cycles – scattering seeds

Class 5N have been studying the ways in which seeds are spread in the environment. They found out that seeds like dandelions and thistle seeds are spread by the wind because they are so light.

Heavy seeds must spread in a different way.

The investigation

The class made a collection of tree seeds.

sycamore seeds   ash seeds

acorns   conkers

The children thought of an investigation.

They wanted to drop the seed from high up and see if the wind from a fan would make the seed float away.

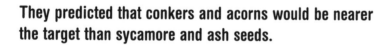

The children tried to drop the seed onto a target. They measured how far away from the target the seed had been blown by the wind from the fan.

They predicted that conkers and acorns would be nearer the target than sycamore and ash seeds.

Here are their results:

	Distance from target (cm)		
	drop 1	drop 2	drop 3
acorn	5	16	9
conker	4	7	4
sycamore	30	35	25
ash	35	45	40

Approaching the investigation

1 **What did the class want to find out?**
They wanted to see which seed was affected most by the wind.

2 **How did they create a fair test?**
They dropped each seed from the same height and tried to drop it onto the target.

3 **How did they carry out the test?**
One person stood on a chair. They tested one seed at a time. They held each seed at the same height and dropped it. They measured how far away from the target each seed fell. They did each test three times.

4 **What did they predict?**
The lighter seeds will be blown more than the heavy seeds.

5 **Was their prediction correct?**
Yes. The acorns and conkers were closer to the target so were not blown so much.

6 **What did they find out?**
Light seeds are most affected by wind.

1

a) List the things they needed to carry out the investigation.

b) Complete the table by working out an average (mean) for each type of seed.

1)

2)

3)

		drop 1	drop 2	drop 3	average
acorn		5	16	9	
conker		4	7	4	
sycamore		30	35	25	
ash		35	45	40	

2

a) Which type of seed was most affected by the wind from the fan?

b) Which type of seed was least affected by the wind from the fan?

c) Why did the class do each drop three times?

3

Use the results above to complete this chart.
Use the average distance from the target for each seed type.

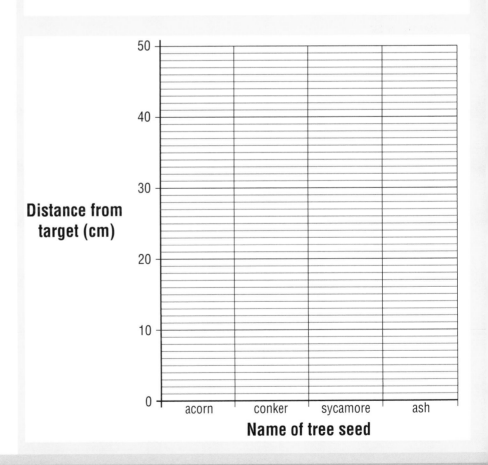

Distance from target (cm) — Name of tree seed

Investigate! Hints and tips

★ You could use a fan heater with the heat turned off to make a breeze.

★ Perhaps you could use three different seeds of each kind to make sure you have not got a freak seed.

Life cycles – summary

Germination

Read this paragraph about seeds. Then write a glossary entry next to each word.
(A glossary is a list of words with their definitions, in alphabetical order.)

Most seeds germinate in the warmth and dampness of spring. If they sprouted in autumn they would have to survive through the cold and darkness of winter. To stop them sprouting too early some seeds need to suffer a period of cold before they will sprout. Coconuts are huge seeds from palm trees and some will only sprout after they have been soaked in salt water for a time. Some seeds will only sprout after they have been through the gut of an animal. This makes sure they have been moved away from the place they grew. Some seeds do not sprout straight away and can lie dormant for years. In a desert seeds lie dormant until rain comes.

GLOSSARY

coconut	
desert	
dormant	
germinate	
gut	

Tick here if you can do this now!

☐ I can make careful observations.   ☐ I can use results to draw conclusions.

☐ I can represent data in charts.   ☐ I can suggest explanations for conclusions reached.

☐ I can relate observations and conclusions to scientific understanding.

Did you know?

★ Some seeds need fire to help them germinate! Seeds of trees and bushes in the Australian desert lie dormant for years waiting for fire to burn away the bushes and trees. This gives room for new plants to grow.

Scattering seeds

Acorns are too heavy to be moved by wind. If they simply rolled away after falling from the tree, oaks would only grow in the bottom of valleys. Acorns and other heavy seeds need animals to move them around. Squirrels and some birds like to eat acorns and will bury a store to last them though the winter. During the winter some of the animals that buried the acorns die or forget where they buried their store and some of these acorns germinate and grow into oak trees.

Apples have a different way of scattering their seed. Animals eat their fleshy fruit and the seeds pass through the animal's gut unharmed. The apple seeds are moved to a new place. They grow away from their parent tree.

Some seeds are covered in tiny hooks. They grip on to the fur of passing animals. They are later rubbed off by the animals and grow in a new place. Goosegrass is like this. Children call it sticky grass because the hooks stick to your clothes.

1 Name a seed that is covered in hooks.
2 Which animals like to eat acorns?
3 How are apple seeds moved long distances?
4 Make a list of some other fruits that animals like to eat.

5 Would it be good for oak trees if there were no squirrels or acorn-eating birds?
6 Would it be good for oak trees if squirrels had perfect memories?

Tick here if you can do this now!

☐ I can make predictions.

☐ I can use results to draw conclusions.

☐ I can represent data in charts.

☐ I can make careful measurements.

☐ I can repeat measurements.

☐ I can draw conclusions.

Gases around us – evaporation

Class 5N have been studying the way that water evaporates. They put bowls of water in different places. The children noticed that water evaporated more quickly if the dishes were left in warm places.

The investigation

The class wanted to see how fast water evaporated from different sized dishes.

Mr Newton set up three dishes. He put them all in the same place.

All the dishes were circular so the children measured the diameter of each dish.

The children poured 200 ml of water into each dish. This meant that some dishes were nearly full but others were less than half full.

Most of the children predicted that the wider dish would evaporate most quickly.

Here are the results:

Dish	Diameter of the dish (cm)	Starting volume of water (ml)	Volume of water (ml) left after 4 days	Volume of water (ml) left after 7 days	Volume of water (ml) left after 10 days
A	5	200	170	160	150
B	8	200	150	130	120
C	12	200	130	100	80

Approaching the investigation

1 **What did the class want to find out?**
They wanted to see how quickly water evaporated from different sized dishes.

2 **How did they create a fair test?**
They put the same amount of water in each one. They put them all in the same place.

3 **How did they carry out the test?**
They measured 200 ml of water and poured that amount into each dish. They put the dishes in the same place. After 4 days they poured the water out of each in turn and measured it. They poured the same water back into each dish.

4 **What did they predict would happen?**
They predicted that the water in the widest dish would evaporate most quickly. They thought it was because there was a bigger surface area.

5 **How did they record their results?**
In a table with space for recording every few days.

6 **What did they find out?**
They found out that the water in the widest dish did evaporate most quickly. They were surprised to see that the rate of evaporation slowed down after the first few days.

7 **Why do you think this is so?**
It might be because the temperature changed, or that the water went well below the rim so breezes would not help to evaporate the water.

1

a) Was the children's prediction correct?

☐ Yes   ☐ No

b) Did the same amount of water evaporate on each day?

2

a) Would it be fair if one of the dishes had a cover on it?

☐ Yes   ☐ No

b) Explain your answer.

c) Which factor did the children change?

d) Which factors did the children keep the same?
Write two factors.

1)

2)

e) What did the children measure?
Write two things.

1)

2)

3

Use the results on page 20 to complete a line graph for Dish A.

First plot the points, then join the points with a line. Label the line 'Dish A'.

Then do the same for the Dish B and Dish C.

Don't forget to label the lines.

Investigate! Hints and tips

★ Use measuring jugs to measure the water volume.

★ Make sure you measure accurately. Close one eye when measuring and get your eye in line with the scale.

★ Make sure that you do not spill any water.

★ Look how far below the rim the water level reaches. This makes a big difference to the evaporation.

Gases around us – gases spread

Class 5N have been studying how quickly gases spread through the air.

The investigation

Class 5N found out that when they put some strong perfume on a saucer the smell spread around the classroom quite quickly.

They decided that this was because the liquid perfume turned to a gas and spread through the air.

They tried to see if some air fresheners evaporated more quickly than others.

Mr Newton had three kinds of air fresheners. He put them on his desk. The children thought the lemon one would spread quickest.

He opened one of the air fresheners and started a timer. The children wrote the time when they smelled the air freshener. Later he covered the freshener and opened one with a different smell.

He did the same with the third one.

The children compared their results in groups of three.

Here are the results:

> The numbers show how many seconds it took for each person to smell each air freshener.

	Jon	Kerrie	Ben
flower smell	40 seconds	40 seconds	45 seconds
fresh pine	30 seconds	35 seconds	35 seconds
lemon zest	50 seconds	60 seconds	70 seconds

Approaching the investigation

1. **What did the class want to find out?**
   They wanted to see which air freshener spread out most quickly.

2. **How did they create a fair test?**
   They opened the air fresheners in the same place, in the same way and the children stayed in the same place.

3. **What equipment did they use?**
   Air freshener
   Timer

4. **How did they carry out the test?**
   They opened the air fresheners one by one. They timed how quickly each person smelled each air freshener.

5. **What did they predict would happen?**
   They thought the lemon smell would be strongest and spread most quickly.

6. **How did they record their results?**
   In a table.

7. **What did they find out?**
   They found out that on average the fresh pine spread quickest. They also noticed that the same person smelled the freshener first each time.

Investigate! Hints and tips

If you complete an investigation like this:
★ Decide what factor you are measuring.

★ You could measure the time taken for one person to smell two different air fresheners.

★ Do this in a place where there is little air movement.
★ Find out what effect a fan has on the results.

1

a) Was the children's prediction correct?

☐ Yes   ☐ No

b) In the test on the opposite page what were the class measuring?

c) In the test what did the children try to keep the same each time?

2

Complete this table by filling in the average for each smell.
The first one has been done for you.

	Jon	Kerrie	Ben	Average
flower smell	40 seconds	40 seconds	46 seconds	42
fresh pine	30 seconds	35 seconds	35 seconds	
lemon zest	50 seconds	60 seconds	70 seconds	

3

Use the average results you calculated in question 2 to complete this bar chart.

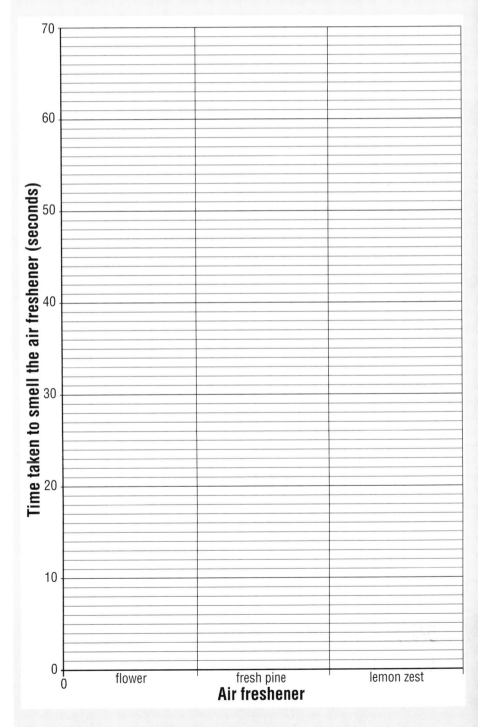

Time taken to smell the air freshener (seconds)

flower   fresh pine   lemon zest

Air freshener

Gases around us – summary

Rate of evaporation

1 Write down the volume of water in each of these jugs:

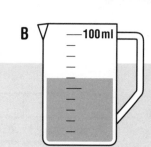

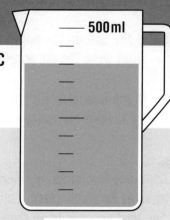

2 If you had about 25 ml of water, which jug would you use?

I would use jug [____] Explain your idea. [____]

Complete this paragraph about evaporation.

We are surrounded by air. Air is a mixture of [_____]. One of the most important gases in air is water [_____]. It is invisible. The amount of water vapour in the air is very changeable. In the Amazon jungle there is lots of [_____] vapour in the air – that is what makes it so sweaty and sticky. In deserts there is hardly any water vapour in the air. This makes it very [_____]. Dry air does not let bodies rot easily. That is one reason why mummies in [_____] are so well-preserved.

We hang washing on a [_____] so that it will dry quickly. The best drying conditions are [_____] and windy days.

Tick here if you can do this now!

☐ I can make careful measurements.

☐ I can repeat measurements.

☐ I can relate observations and conclusions to scientific understanding.

☐ I can use results to draw conclusions.

☐ I can suggest explanations for conclusions reached.

☐ I can evaluate the evidence and the activity.

Did you know?

★ The air in Peru is very dry. People who live there can dry potatoes so they keep for a long time.

Gases spread

Our noses detect smells. Some animals have an amazing sense of smell. We use dogs to sniff out bombs and drugs in airports. Dogs can use their sense of smell to find people buried under rubble in earthquakes. Pigs also have a great sense of smell. In France they are used to sniff out truffles, which are very valuable mushrooms. Moths have the best sense of smell in the world. A male moth can smell a female moth over five kilometres away!

The smell from warm perfume spreads more quickly than when it is cold. When perfume is dabbed onto skin it is warmed up and so spreads quickly. Perfumed candles work as the perfume is heated by the candle flame.

1   What jobs do dogs do in earthquake disasters?

2   What jobs do dogs do in airports?

3   Which animals have the best sense of smell?

4   Explain why perfume on the skin will be smelled more quickly than perfume on clothes.

5   Which of these sentences is true? Tick one.
    ☐ *You can only smell perfume when it evaporates.*
    ☐ *You can smell the liquid perfume.*

Tick here if you can do this now!

☐ I can make predictions.

☐ I can use results to draw conclusions.

☐ I can draw conclusions.

☐ I can make careful measurements.

☐ I can represent data in charts.

☐ I can suggest explanations for conclusions reached.

Did you know?

★ The gas we use in our cookers does not naturally have a smell. This is added to the gas so that people can detect even the smallest gas leaks.

Changing state – melting

Class 5N have been studying the way in which ice cubes can be kept solid in different conditions.

The investigation

Class 5N found out that ice cubes put into warm water melted much more quickly than ice cubes put into cold water.

They decided that materials changed from solid to liquid more quickly if they are warm.

They investigated the effect of wrapping the ice cubes in layers of cloth.

- They timed how long it took for all the solid ice to turn to liquid water.
- They made sure the cubes were all the same size.
- They made sure all the cubes were put in the same place.
- They used the same cloth for each cube.

Here are the results:

	Time taken to melt completely
no covering	30 minutes
one layer of cloth	45 minutes
two layers of cloth	50 minutes
three layers of cloth	60 minutes
four layers of cloth	75 minutes

Approaching the investigation

1 What did the class want to find out?
If wrapping ice cubes with different numbers of layers of cloth changed melting time.

2 How did they create a fair test?
They made sure the cubes were the same size and they were all put in the same place. They used the same cloth to wrap the ice cubes.

3 What equipment did they use?
Timer
Cloth
Ice cubes

4 What factor did they measure?
The time it took to melt each cube.

5 How did they record their results?
They used a table to record their results.

6 What did they find out?
The more layers covering the ice cube the slower it melted.

7 Why do you think this is so?
Layers of cloth insulate the ice cube from the warmth of the classroom. Thicker layers of material stopped the heat of the room travelling to the cubes.

Investigate! Hints and tips

★ Do not look too often at the cubes to see if they are solid. Look only every 10 minutes.

★ If you have a data logger attach it to the computer and record the changes of temperature as the ice melts.

The class now want to test which material would keep the ice cubes solid longest.

They decide to use bubble wrap, aluminium foil, a towel, newspaper and a plastic bag.

They time how long each cube stays solid.

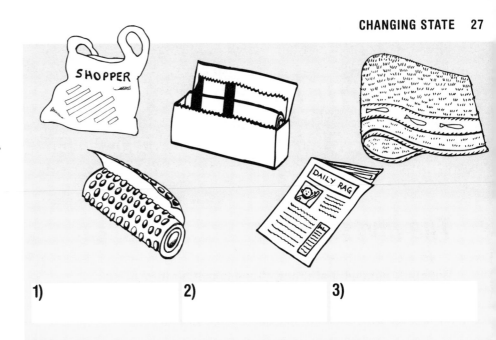

1

List the things needed to carry out this investigation

1)

2)

3)

2

a) What factor will they measure?

b) What factor will they change?

c) How do they keep the test fair?

3

Use the results on page 26 to complete this bar chart.

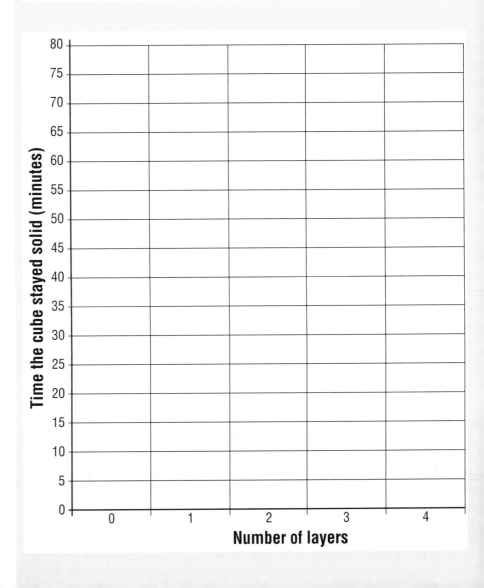

Changing state – condensation

Class 5N have been studying the way in which condensation forms on very cold surfaces.

The investigation

The class noticed that drops of condensation formed on the outside of cans from the fridge. They also noticed it formed on the outside of glasses of cold drinks.

They wanted to see if the temperature inside the can made a difference to the amount of condensation on the outside.

- In can 1 they put ice and salt.
- In can 2 they put ice and a little cold water.
- In can 3 they put ice and lots of cold water.
- In can 4 they put cold water.

They used a thermometer to test the temperature inside each can.

They asked three children from another class to say which can had the most drops on outside of the can. Lots of ticks equals lots of drops!

Here are the results:

Can number	Temperature inside can	Amount of condensation after 5 minutes
1	–8 °C	✓✓✓✓✓
2	0 °C	✓✓✓
3	3 °C	✓✓
4	12 °C	✓

Approaching the investigation

1 What did the class want to find out?
They wanted to find out if the temperature of the inside of cans made a difference to the number of drops of water formed on the outside of cold cans.

2 What did they do to make the test fair?
They used the same cans and put the same number and size of ice cubes in each.
They asked children from another class to judge the amount of water on the outside.

3 What equipment did they use?
Thermometer
Cans
Ice cubes
Cold water
Salt

4 How did they carry out the test?
They put different mixtures of ice, salt and water into cans.

5 What did they find out?
They noticed that more drops formed on the outside of the coldest can.

6 Why do you think this is so?
Condensation occurs most on cold surfaces.

Investigate! Hints and tips

★ Make sure you read the temperature on the thermometer correctly. Get your head in line to do the reading properly.

★ Use containers of equal size.
★ When judging the amount of condensation ask another person to help.

The class tried another investigation. They wanted to see if the type of container had an effect on the amount of condensation. They used four different containers: a polystyrene cup, a metal can, a plastic beaker and a glass jar. They used the same mixture of salt and ice which had made the cans so cold.

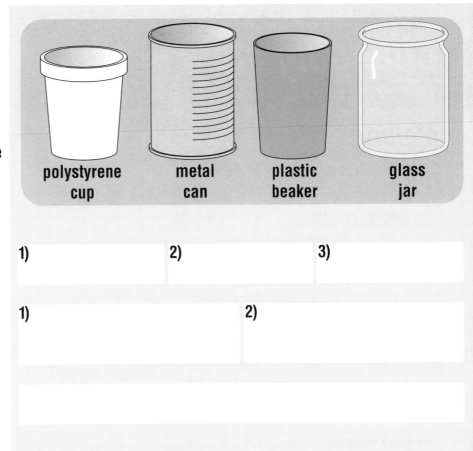

polystyrene cup   metal can   plastic beaker   glass jar

a) List three things needed to carry out this investigation.

1)

2)

3)

b) Write two factors the children need to keep the same in this test.

1)

2)

c) What will the children be measuring?

a) Predict which container will have the most condensation.

b) Explain your idea.

3 Use the results on page 28 to complete this chart.

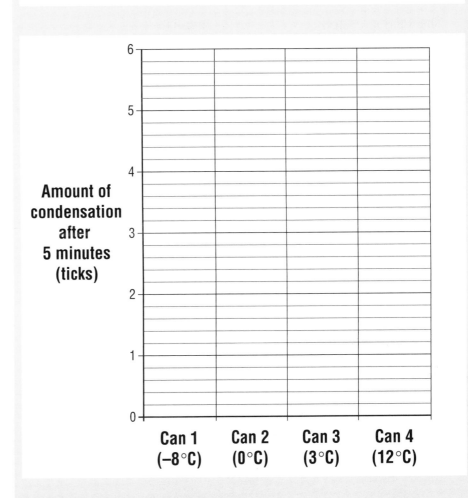

Amount of condensation after 5 minutes (ticks)

Can 1 (−8°C)   Can 2 (0°C)   Can 3 (3°C)   Can 4 (12°C)

Changing state – summary

Melting

Complete this paragraph about melting.

The freezing point of [_____] is 0 °C. When ice cubes get above freezing point they [_____]. We can keep ice cubes solid for a long time in a thermos flask. The flask is made so that very little [_____] from the room gets into the flask. The inside of the flask is made of silver coated glass.

The glass is made of two layers like a double glazed window. This is better than a single layer of [_____] at stopping heat getting into the flask.

The lid stops warm [_____] getting into the flask.

Tick here if you can do this now!

- ☐ I can make careful observations.
- ☐ I can represent data in charts.
- ☐ I can suggest explanations for conclusions reached.
- ☐ I can use results to draw conclusions.
- ☐ I can identify patterns in results.
- ☐ I can evaluate the evidence and the activity.

Did you know?

★ In Victorian times before there were fridges, ice was taken from lakes in the winter and stored in ice houses. These were underground buildings where the ice stayed solid all through the summer. Rich people would use this ice in summer to make cool drinks to impress their friends.

The water cycle

Most of our water falls in the form of rain or snow.

- It starts in the seas and oceans.
- Liquid water evaporates to form water vapour.
- This condenses to form clouds.

The drops of liquid water in clouds are tiny and are kept up by winds in the cloud.

- Once the drops have got large enough they fall from the clouds as rain, hail or snow.

- The water then finds its way back to the seas and oceans in rivers and streams.

Fog is cloud which is touching the ground. It is often caused where damp air is in contact with very cold ground.

Is the water in clouds liquid or vapour?

Draw a diagram to show this water cycle of evaporation and condensation.

Tick here if you can do this now!

- ☐ I can turn ideas into a form that can be investigated.
- ☐ I can make careful observations.
- ☐ I can suggest explanations.
- ☐ I can evaluate the evidence and the activity.

- ☐ I can make predictions.
- ☐ I can use results to draw conclusions.
- ☐ I can understand science.

Did you know?

⭐ Condensation happens all the time in fridges and freezers. The water turns to ice where it is very cold.

Earth, Sun and Moon – length of shadows

Class 5N have been studying the way in which the shadows made by the Sun change during the day.

The investigation

Class 5N found out that during the day the position of shadows changes.

They noticed that the length of the shadow also changes.
- When the Sun is high in the sky the shadows are short.
- When the Sun is low in the sky the shadows are long.

The children used a skittle to make a shadow. They decided to measure the length of the shadow at different times of the day. They used a clock to tell the correct time. The children predicted that the shadows would get shorter towards lunchtime and then get longer during the afternoon.

Here are the results:

Time	Length of shadow (cm)
9·00 a.m.	55
10·00	35
11·00	20
12·00 p.m.	10
1·00	15
2·00	20
3·00	30

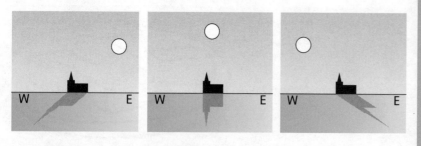

Approaching the investigation

1 What did the class want to find out?
They wanted to see if shadows made by the Sun change during the day.

2 What equipment did they use?
Skittle to make shadow.
Ruler to measure shadow.
Clock to tell correct time.

3 What did they predict would happen?
They thought the shadow would get shorter until midday and then get longer during the afternoon.

4 What factor did they keep the same in each test?
The skittle.
The position of the skittle.

5 What factor did they change in each test?
The time.

6 What factor did they measure each time?
The length of the shadow.

7 What did they find out?
They noticed that the length of the shadow changed during the day.

8 Why do you think this is so?
The Sun appears to move across the sky as the Earth rotates on its axis. The Sun is highest in the sky at midday and this makes the shadows shortest. When the Sun is low in the sky the shadows are long.

1

One of the children said she thought the shadows would be longest just before sunset.

a) Do you think she is right?

☐ Yes ☐ No

b) Explain your idea.

2

a) The children then gave a reason for the changing shadows. Which child is right?

Tick one: ☐ The shadows change as the Sun moves round the Earth.
☐ The shadows change as the Earth turns on its axis.
☐ The shadows change because of the Sun.

b) Which of these rough graphs shows the correct results?

Tick one:

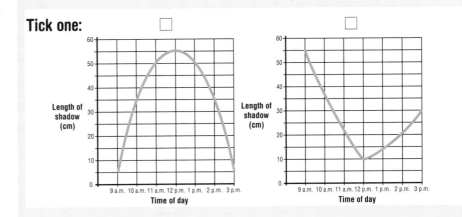

3

Use the results on page 32 to complete this graph.
Put crosses to mark the length of the shadow at different times of day.
Join the crosses to make a line graph.

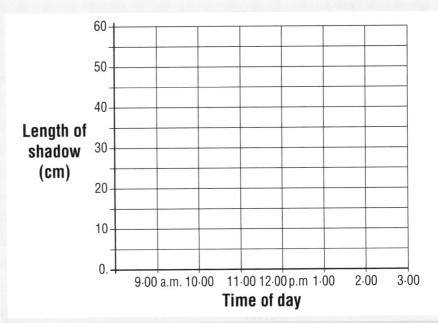

Investigate! Hints and tips

★ If you do an investigation into the length of shadows made by the Sun, work as a class.

★ Find a place indoors or in the playground where the Sun shines all day long and there are no shadows from buildings or tall trees.

★ Weigh down a large sheet of paper and draw the shadow as it appears each hour. Write in the time next to the shadow.

★ Measure the length of the shadow at the end of the day.

Earth, Sun and Moon – sunset times

Class 5N have been studying the time of sunset.

The investigation

Everyone in the class knew that there was longer daylight in the summer than in the winter.

- Jane thought there was a difference of 2 hours in the time of sunset between summer and winter.
- Kate predicted there was more than two hours difference between summer and winter sunset times.

They looked on the Internet to see the times of sunset.

They found out that the time of sunset changed during the year.

They put the times in a table:

	Time of sunset (p.m.)
January	4.20
February	5.20
March	6.10
April	7.10
May	8.00
June	8.30
July	8.20
August	7.30
September	6.20
October	5.10
November	4.15
December	4.00
(All these times ignore the clocks changing for British Summertime)	

Approaching the investigation

1 **What did the class want to find out?**
They wanted to find if the time of sunset changed during the year.

2 **Where did they get their information?**
They used the Internet to look up times of sunset.

3 **Why didn't they find the information for themselves?**
It would have taken all year to work it out.

4 **What did they predict would happen?**
Half the class thought there was a difference of two hours in the time of sunset between summer and winter. The other half predicted there was more than two hours difference between summer and winter sunset times.

5 **What factor were they measuring?**
The time of sunset.

6 **What did they find out?**
They found that the time of sunset got later and later until June. After that it got earlier and earlier until December.

Investigate! Hints and tips

Do this study.

★ Use www.google.co.uk to start your search. Search for *sunset times UK*.
★ You will be able to enter the name of the nearest city in many of the pages. The times shown above are for Birmingham.
★ Make sure that you look at the sunset time for the middle of the month in each case.

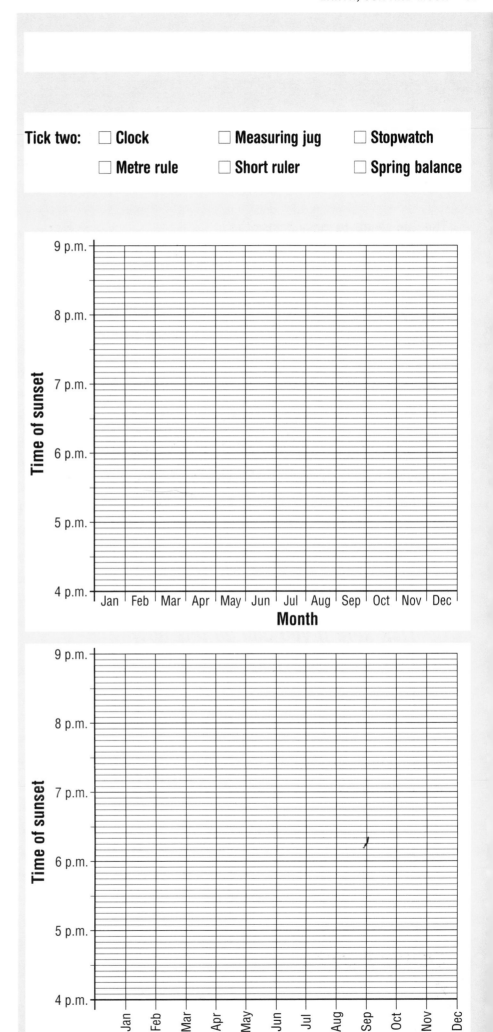

1 Did Jane or Kate make the right prediction?

2 The class wanted to measure shadow length at different times of the year. What measuring instruments would they use?

Tick two: ☐ Clock   ☐ Measuring jug   ☐ Stopwatch
           ☐ Metre rule ☐ Short ruler   ☐ Spring balance

3
a) Use the results on page 34 to complete this bar chart.

b) Use the same results to draw a line graph.

Earth, Sun and Moon – summary

Length of shadows

Complete this paragraph about the Sun.

The Sun seems to move across the _____. In fact it is the _____ which is turning on its axis.

The _____ stays still but appears to move! The Earth _____ but you cannot feel it moving!

This change in the position of the Sun is used to tell the _____ using shadow clocks. The main _____ with shadow clocks in Britain is the amount of cloud we get. In places like Egypt there is much less _____ and shadow clocks are more useful.

Tick here if you can do this now!

- ☐ I can make predictions.
- ☐ I can make careful measurements.
- ☐ I can identify patterns in results.
- ☐ I can suggest explanations.
- ☐ I can make careful observations.
- ☐ I can use results to draw conclusions.
- ☐ I can draw conclusions.
- ☐ I can evaluate the evidence and the activity.

Did you know?

★ The Sun is directly overhead at the Equator on only two days each year. On these days at noon the shadows made by the sun are only as big as the object itself.

Sunset times

Complete this paragraph about sunset times.

In winter we get up in the _____ and go to bed in the dark.

In summer we get up in the _____ and go to bed in the light.

The Sun rises in the _____ and sets in the _____.
This is because the Earth turns on its _____. In Summer the days are _____ and the nights are short.

In _____ the days are short and the nights are long.

In the spring and autumn the days and _____ are about equal in length.

Tick here if you can do this now!

☐ I can make predictions.

☐ I can use results to draw conclusions.

☐ I can identify patterns in results.

☐ I can use scientific understanding.

☐ I can make careful observations.

☐ I can represent data in charts.

☐ I can draw conclusions.

Did you know?

★ At the North and South Poles there is six months of daytime and six months of night-time. On a day in spring the Sun rises and does not set again until a day in autumn six months later. This only happens at the poles themselves, but near the poles there are big differences between the lengths of the days at different times of the year.

Changing sounds – muffling sounds

Class 5N have been studying the way in which sounds can be muffled by different materials.

The investigation

Class 5N wanted to see how far away they could hear a quiet buzzer.

One person had their back to the box so they did not know when the sound was being made.

They moved a metre further away from the box each time.

They put their hand up when they heard the sound.

The children controlling the sound recorded the distance at which the sound was still heard.

They found out that they could hear the buzzer, without any wrapping, up to 45 metres away.

When they wrapped the buzzer in different materials they found that some materials muffled the sound.

They then measured the distance at which they could hear the buzzer when it was wrapped in different materials. Most of the children thought the thick coat would muffle the sound the most.

Here are the results when they tested Rashid:

Material muffling the sound	Number of metres at which sound could still be heard
nothing	45
paper	40
woolly jumper	30
thick coat	20
bags of sand	15

Approaching the investigation

1 **What did the class want to find out?**
They wanted to see which materials muffled the sound best.

2 **How did they create a fair test?**
They made sure the person being tested could not see the buzzer being worked. They used the same person to hear the buzzer and moved a metre away each time.

3 **What equipment did they use?**
A buzzer
Different materials to muffle the sound
Metre stick

4 **What did they predict would happen?**
They though that the thick coat would muffle the sound best.

5 **How did they record their results?**
They measured the number of metres and recorded it in a table.

6 **What did they find out?**
They found out that bags of sand were best at muffling the sound.

7 **Why do you think this is so?**
Sand is heavy and absorbs the sound best.

a) What factor did they change in the investigation?

Tick one: ☐ The distance from the sound   ☐ The covering
          ☐ The sound made by the buzzer   ☐ The person being tested

b) What factors did they keep the same?

Tick two: ☐ The distance from the sound   ☐ The covering
          ☐ The sound made by the buzzer   ☐ The person being tested

c) What factor did they measure?

Tick one: ☐ The distance from the sound   ☐ The covering
          ☐ The sound made by the buzzer   ☐ The person being tested

a) In the test on page 38 was the prediction made by the children correct?

b) Why did the same child always have to measure the distance between the buzzer and the listening person?

Use the results on page 38 to complete this bar chart.

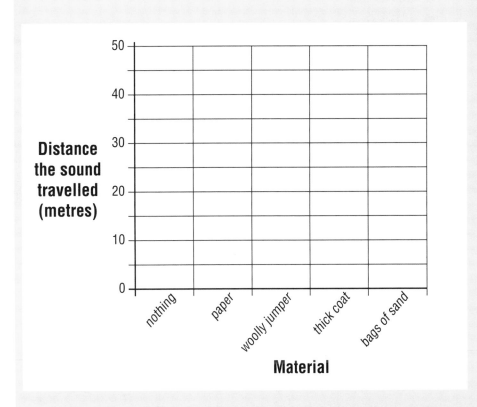

Distance the sound travelled (metres)

Material

Investigate! Hints and tips

★ Work in the playground to do the tests.
★ Try to work on a day when it is not windy.

★ Make sure that the person who is listening to the sounds cannot tell when the sound is being made.
★ Practise making the sound in the same way each time.

Changing sounds – pitch of sounds

Class 5N have been studying the way different objects make different pitched sounds.

The investigation

Class 5N were experimenting with an old guitar. Mr Newton asked them to work out how the guitar makes low pitched sounds and how it made high pitched sounds.

They found out that there were three things that made a sound high pitched:

- tight string
- long string
- thick string

The next thing they tried was to test some ordinary string.

String
The children tested different lengths of string.

They attached weights to the strings. They found that:

- short strings had a high pitch
- strings with a heavy weight attached had a high pitch

Drums
The children then tested the pitch of drums.

They found that:

- small drums had a high pitch
- when they stretched the drum skin the pitch went higher

Tuning forks
The children then tested the pitch of tuning forks.

They found that:

- small forks had a high pitch

Approaching the investigation

1 What did the class want to find out?
What factors affect the pitch of sounds made by different objects.

2 How did they compare things fairly?
They only compared similar things.
- They compared strings with other strings.
- They compared tuning forks with other tuning forks.

3 What equipment did they use?
Old guitar
Strings
Weights
Drums
Tuning forks

4 What did they find out?
Smaller objects have a high pitch. They also found that a tighter tension makes a higher pitch.

1

a) In which tests did the children change three factors?

Tick two: ☐ guitar strings   ☐ tuning forks
           ☐ string   ☐ drums

b) Which test had only one factor?

Tick one: ☐ guitar strings   ☐ tuning forks
           ☐ string   ☐ drums

2

You have a large glass jar and a small glass jar.

a) Predict which glass will make the higher pitch sound when you tap them.

Tick one: ☐ large glass jar   ☐ small glass jar

b) Explain your idea.

3

Suggest another investigation of the different pitch of sounds.

Investigate! Hints and tips

Make your own pitched instrument.
(Ask an adult for help with cutting.)
★ Get a piece of wood about the size of a book.
★ Cut six pieces of string to different lengths.

★ Attach each piece of string to the wood using drawing pins. Make sure the string is pulled tight.
★ Pluck the strings to listen to your instrument.

Changing sounds – summary

Muffling sounds

1 Noisy neighbours are a real problem. Thick walls are a good way to stop the sound travelling from one house to another. If the noise is coming from a flat above suggest one thing that might help.

2 Noisy roads are a problem. Much of the noise comes through the glass of the windows. Double glazing in house windows cuts down the noise. Suggest one reason why double glazing cuts down noise.

3 *Fill in the blanks in this paragraph.*

People working noisy machinery have _____ protectors.
The material inside the protector _____ the sound.
If workers do not use ear protectors their hearing gets worse
and they may become _____ . Some singers in pop
groups use ear protectors because their music is so _____ .

Tick here if you can do this now!

- [ ] I can turn ideas into a form that can be investigated.
- [ ] I can identify patterns in results.
- [ ] I can relate observations and conclusions to scientific understanding.
- [ ] I can make predictions.
- [ ] I can represent data in charts.
- [ ] I can suggest explanations for conclusions reached.

Did you know?

★ The loudest sound ever recorded was when the volcano Krakatoa blew up in Indonesia. It could be heard thousands of kilometres away in Australia.

Pitch of sounds

Bats use very high pitched sounds to help them find their way around. The sound is reflected off objects back to the bat's large and sensitive ears. The bat uses the sound echoes to build up a picture of its surroundings. Underwater dolphins use high pitched sounds to track their prey in murky water. Like bats they use the echoes to help them find their way.

As people get older they find it harder to hear very high pitched sounds. This means that very young children can hear sounds that adults cannot hear. Many children can hear some of the noise made by bats but adults are deaf to these squeaks.

High pitched sounds are used by doctors to make a picture of the inside of someone's body. This is called 'ultrasound' and is used a great deal to check unborn babies inside their mother's body.

1 There are three paragraphs above. Write a title for each paragraph.

2 Underline in red the names of the animals that use high pitched sound.

3 Underline in blue the single word that describes very high pitched sounds.

4 Which is most like the way that bats use sound? Tick one of these:

☐ The bat listens to the reflections of its own sound.

☐ The bat listens to the sound of its own surroundings.

Tick here if you can do this now!

☐ I can make predictions.

☐ I can use results to draw conclusions.

☐ I can draw conclusions.

☐ I can make careful observations.

☐ I can identify patterns in results.

☐ I can suggest explanations for conclusions reached.

Did you know?

★ The opposite of 'ultrasound' is 'infrasound'. This is sound which is so low pitched that we cannot hear it at all. Elephants make infrasound to communicate with each other.

Answers

Page 9

a) Tick: skipping

b) Tick: Laura's pulse rate was 80 beats per minute when sitting.

c) Tick: Walking up and down stairs for one minute.

d) Walking up stairs is harder exercise than walking on the flat. Harder exercise makes your pulse rate go higher.

a) Jon's pulse rate was lower than Laura's after any of the activities.

b) 1) Jon's pulse rate went higher as the exercise got harder.
   2) The gap between Jon and Laura's pulse rate was larger the harder the exercise.

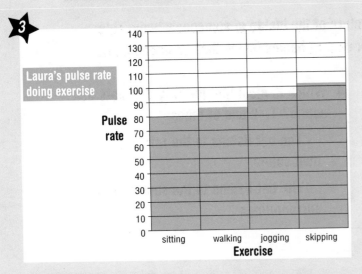

Page 11

a) Teri

b) The longer you do the survey, the more accurate the results.

a) Circle: No

b) One grape is much smaller than one apple. It would be fairer to compare one apple with a few grapes.

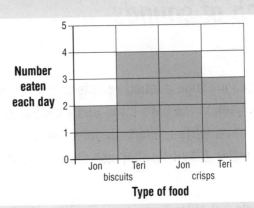

Page 12

You feel a beat of your pulse each time your HEART beats.

Your heart pumps BLOOD around the body.

Your heart beats FASTER when you exercise because you need oxygen and energy in your muscles. The OXYGEN is taken from your lungs. Energy comes from the FOOD you eat. It is taken by the BLOOD to all parts of your body.

Different people have different PULSE rates. Part of the reason for this is fitness. Very fit people have low pulse rates. This is because their HEART pumps lots of blood each time it BEATS. It takes time for pulse rates to go back to NORMAL after exercise. Very FIT people will go back to a slow pulse rate very QUICKLY.

Page 13

★ Biscuits are made with a lot of <u>fat</u> and <u>sugar</u>.

★ Crisps are made with a lot of <u>fat</u> and <u>salt</u>.

★ Too much fat can make us <u>overweight</u>.

★ Too much sugar can make our <u>teeth decay</u>.

4 crisps

5 bicuits

TITLES SHOULD MENTION HEALTHY EATING OR DOCTORS' ADVICE

Most doctors think that we should eat more fruit and vegetables. There are several reasons for this. Fruit and vegetables have lots of fibre to keep your (intestines) working properly. They have lots of vitamins to keep (skin) healthy. They fill you up but will not make you fat.

TITLES SHOULD MENTION FOODS TO TAKE CARE WITH

Biscuits and crisps are tasty but we should only eat a few of them. Crisps and biscuits both have a lot of fat in them. Eating fat can make us overweight. Biscuits contain lots of sugar, which may also make us overweight. The salt in crisps makes us thirsty, causes our (kidneys) to work very hard and might cause poor health as we get older.

Page 15

a) Tick: warm

b) 7 days

a) The class could place a pea and a bean in compost in a warm cupboard. They could then check to see which germinated quickest.

b) The compost, where the pot was placed, the size of the pot and the amount of water.

c) How quickly each seed germinated.

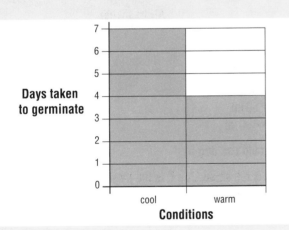

Page 17

a) Four seeds, a chair, a target (a piece of paper to use as a target)

b) acorn – 10 cm, conker – 5 cm, sycamore – 30 cm, ash – 40 cm
Calculated by adding the distance for each seed and dividing by 3.

a) Ash seed

b) Conker

c) To make sure the results were accurate.

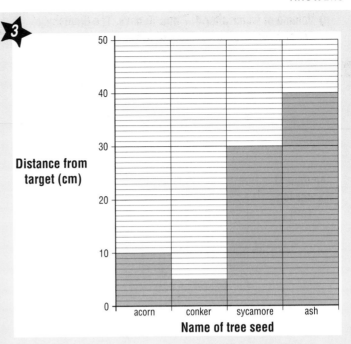

Page 18

coconut	a large nut with a hairy shell, white flesh and milky juice
desert	an area of land that has almost no water or rain and few plants
dormant	inactive, sleeping
germinate	when a seed starts to grow
gut	another word for stomach

Page 19

1 Goosegrass

2 Squirrels and birds

3 They are eaten by animals and pass through the animal's gut.

4 Plums, bananas, strawberries or another fruit you can think of

5 No

6 No

Page 21

a) Tick: Yes

b) No, less water evaporated after 4 days.

a) Tick: No

b) If one of the dishes has a cover on it, water would not evaporate from it as quickly as the other two dishes.

c) The diameter of the dish.

d) Starting volume of water and where the dishes were placed.

e) Volume of water after 4, 7 and 10 days. The diameter of the dish, the starting volume of water.

★3

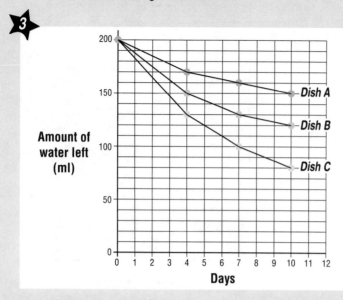

Page 23

★1

a) Tick: No

b) How quickly gases spread through the air.

c) The distance between the air freshener and the class.

★2

a) Fresh pine – 33 seconds, Lemon zest – 60 seconds.

★3

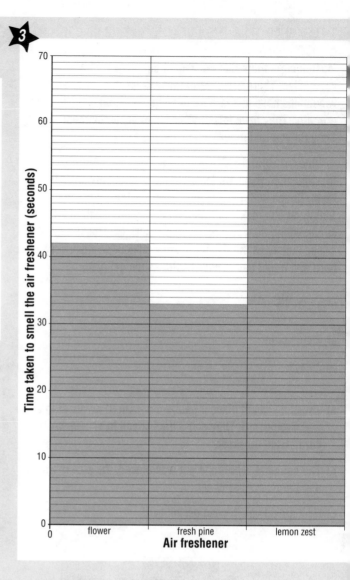

Page 24

1   A – 8 ml
    B – 60 ml
    C – 400 ml

2   I would use Jug B.

Jug A is too small. Jug C is too large and the capacity would be too difficult to read.

We are surrounded by air. Air is a mixture of GASES. One of the most important gases in air is water VAPOUR. It is invisible. The amount of water vapour in the air is very changeable. In the Amazon jungle there is lots of WATER vapour in the air – that is what makes it so sweaty and sticky. In deserts there is hardly any water vapour in the air. This makes it very DRY. Dry air does not let bodies rot easily. That is one reason why mummies in EGYPT are so well-preserved.

We hang washing on a LINE so that it will dry quickly. The best drying conditions are HOT and windy days.

Page 25

1 Dogs search for people buried in earthquakes by smelling them.

2 Dogs search for drugs and bombs in airports.

3 Moths

4 Warmer perfume spreads more quickly than colder perfume. Perfume on skin is warmer than on clothes.

5 We can only smell perfume when it evaporates.

Page 27

Ice cubes, different coverings, timer.

a) Which covering is the best insulator.

b) The type of covering.

c) They could make sure all the ice cubes were the same size.

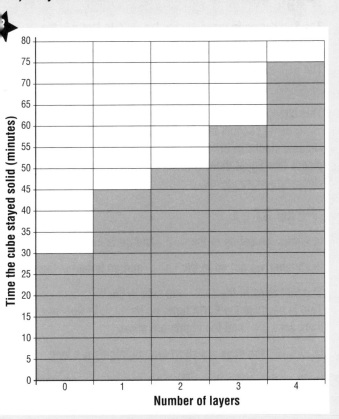

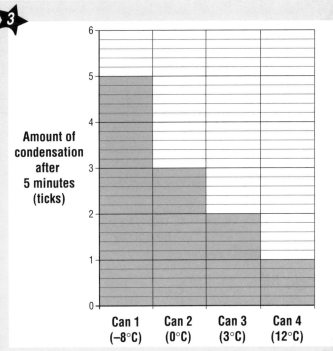

Page 30

The freezing point of WATER is 0 °C. When ice cubes get above freezing point they MELT. We can keep ice cubes solid for a long time in a thermos flask. The flask is made so that very little HEAT from the room gets into the flask. The inside of the flask is made of silver coated glass.

The glass is made of two layers like a double glazed window. This is better than a single layer of GLASS at stopping heat getting into the flask.

The lid stops warm AIR getting into the flask.

Page 31

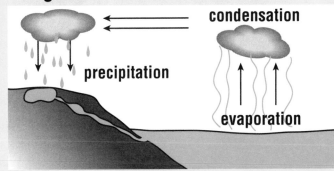

Page 29

a) The different containers, salt and ice, a thermometer.

b) The ice and salt mixture, the amount of ice and salt and the size of the container.

c) How much condensation is on the outside of each container after 5 minutes.

a) The metal can.

b) Metal is a good thermal conductor so will cool the quickest. More condensation forms because it is colder than the other containers. The water vapour condenses as it touches the cold surface.

Page 33

a) Tick: Yes

b) Just before sunset, the Sun is lowest in the sky. A low Sun in the sky makes long shadows.

a) Tick: The shadows change as the Earth turns on its axis.

b) Tick the graph on the right.

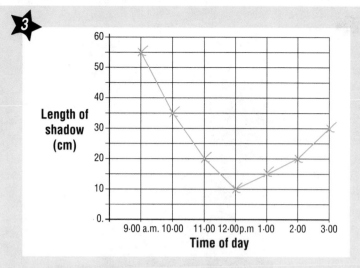

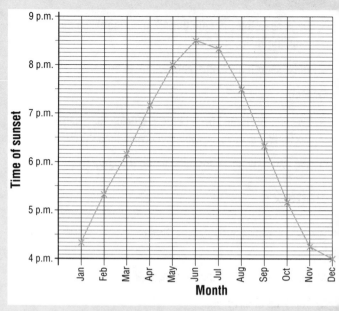

Page 35

Kate was right.

2 Tick: Metre rule and Clock

3

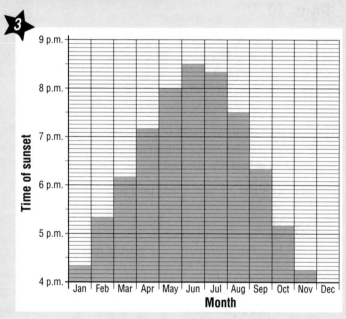

Page 36

The Sun seems to move across the SKY. In fact it is the EARTH which is turning on its axis.

The SUN stays still but appears to move! The Earth ROTATES but you cannot feel it moving!

This change in the position of the Sun is used to tell the TIME using shadow clocks. The main PROBLEM with shadow clocks in Britain is the amount of cloud we get. In places like Egypt there is much less CLOUD and shadow clocks are more useful.

Page 37

In winter we get up in the DARK and go to bed in the dark.

In summer we get up in the LIGHT and go to bed in the light.

The Sun rises in the EAST and sets in the WEST.
This is because the Earth turns on its AXIS. In Summer the days are LONG and the nights are short.

In WINTER the days are short and the nights are long.

In the spring and autumn the days and NIGHTS are about equal in length.

Page 39

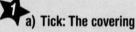
a) Tick: The covering

b) Tick: The sound made by the buzzer and the person being tested.

c) Tick: The distance from the buzzer.

a) No

b) The same person listened for the buzzer each time because some people have more sensitive hearing than others.